# CHOOSE

# FAITH

## OVER

# FEAR

Gaining Victory In Times
of Uncertainties

Livingstone O. Bankole

CHOOSE FAITH OVER FEAR
[Gaining Victory In Times of Uncertainties]
Copyright © 2021 by **Livingstone O. Bankole**

Unless otherwise indicated, Bible quotations are taken from King James Version. Copyright © 1988 by B. B. Kirkbride Bible Company. Encarta World English Dictionary 1998 - 2004 Microsoft Corporation.

ISBN 13: 978-1-7343991-3-4

**EDITED BY: ESTHER ODULAJA**
**PUBLISHED BY: Platform for Success Press**

+1 917 826 3566, info@pacetas.com

**FOR ALL INVITATIONS & ORDERING INFORMATION:**
CHRIST EVANGELISTIC MISSIONS MINISTRIES A.K.A LIVINGSTONE BANKOLE WORLD EVANGELISM MINISTRIES(LBWEM) NYC, USA.

EMAILS: evangelistbankole @gmail.com,
godliness1000@hotmail.com

TELEPHONE: +1 (917) 937-8944

THANKS FOR YOUR PATRONAGE AND CONSIDERATIONS. GOD BLESS YOU IN JESUS MERCIFUL AND AWESOME NAME, AMEN!!!

# CHOOSE
# FAITH
## OVER
# FEAR

Livingstone O. Bankole

LITERATURE CRUSADING MINISTRY.

MORE THAN 5-BILLION SOULS HOLY GHOST CRUSADES:

INVITATIONS TO EVENTS, PROGRAMS, CHURCHES, AND HOLY GHOST CRUSADES FOR TOWNS, CITIES, AND NATIONS WORLDWIDE.

EVANGELIST LIVINGSTONE OLALEKAN BANKOLE HAS A MANDATE FROM GOD TO REACH MORE THAN 5-BILLION SOULS FOR THE LORD JESUS CHRIST BEFORE THE RAPTURE OR ASCENSION OF THE SAINTS OF GOD MOST HIGH, AND THE SECOND COMING OF JESUS CHRIST, THROUGH HOLY GHOST CRUSADES!

YOU CAN SEND YOUR INVITATIONS FOR HOLY GHOST CRUSADES TO HIS MINISTRIES @ CHRIST EVANGELISTIC MISSIONS MINISTRIES A.K.A LIVINGSTONE BANKOLE

WORLD EVANGELISM MINISTRIES (LBWEM) NYC, USA.

## CONTACT INFORMATION:

EMAILS: evangelistbankole @gmail.com

OR godliness1000@hotmail.com

TELEPHONE: +1 (917) 937-8944

THANKS FOR YOUR PATRONAGE AND CONSIDERATIONS.

GOD BLESS YOU IN JESUS' MERCIFUL AND AWESOME NAME, AMEN!!!

# TABLE OF CONTENTS

✦

# DEDICATION

✦

I dedicate this book to my wife, OMONIYI BANKOLE. She is indeed a woman of faith over fear! She is an Intercessor by the HOLY GHOST'S grace and mercies.

Thank you, my Love, for your support and sound encouragement! God bless our union in Jesus' mighty name, Amen!

# 1

❧

# FAITH

*"Now faith is the substance of things hoped for,
the evidence of things not seen."*

**Hebrews 11:1**

God has unlimited resources available to every believer in His heavenly Kingdom. But the big question is; how can we tap into God's divine virtues from the earthly realm? And it heightens when you begin to wonder: how do I consistently and unreservedly partake of God's promises for my life?

Just like the horizon marks the meeting point of the sky and land; faith signifies the line that links the natural and the supernatural! Faith enables every believer to access their inheritance in Christ Jesus. It releases miracles, healings, deliverances, and breakthroughs!

Faith in God delivers indescribable solutions to long term problems and puzzles that proved impossible. It can be said as a firm persuasion, assurance, and total confidence in God's faithfulness. Faith is an asset that grants unimaginable and incredible exploits to everyone who believes, *"For with God nothing shall be impossible."* (Luke 1:37)

Are you interested in accessing all that faith in God has to offer? Over the forward pages, I will unveil faith's uniqueness in accelerating you into your divine destiny. You will find out how to make faith work as you walk into your world of possibilities, miracles, signs, and wonders!

Are you ready?

**For a moment, consider how faith is unique …**

## Faith is a spirit

*"We having the same Spirit of faith, according as it is written, I believed, and therefore have I spoken; We also believe, and therefore speak;"*

**2 Corinthians 3:13**

Faith is a Spirit that comes upon a person by the power of God. It enters your spirit by the Spirit of God, enabling you to do exploits in God's kingdom.

## Faith is a gift

> *"For by grace are ye saved through faith; and that not of yourselves: it is the gift of God: Not of works, lest any man should boast."*
> **Ephesians 2: 8-9**

Faith is God's gift to help us believe in the gospel. Beyond that, we also receive God's priceless gift of salvation when we believe. Faith is the bedrock of trust or confidence in God, Jesus Christ, and the Holy Ghost. It also serves as the foundation on which God's doctrine thrive.

Abraham, the father of faith believed in God to solve every mystery around his life. Rest assured, he knew that God was working it out for his good. So, God counted his faith as righteousness for him! Faith is inevitable in a Christian's life.

Abraham believed amid faithless circumstances. His faith is certainly jaw-drop-down awestruck. Have you ever wondered how to establish a strong faith in God? I have provided a few steps to take in living a life filled with faith.

**How to Activate your Faith Life Daily**

- Pray in the Holy Spirit (in tongues) throughout the day.
- Read the Holy Bible and meditate on scriptural texts both in the Old and New testaments.
- Listen to gospel music and remove worldly/secular music or every ungodly music from your view and hearing.
- Involve yourself in Church activities; get busy for Christ or participate in divine works in your Church groups.
- Make godly friends i.e., with people of faith and not unbelievers, do not be unequally yoked with unbelievers.
- Give yourself at least 10 minutes of quiet time alone with the Holy Ghost every day.
- Watch Christian movies and not worldly, violent, secular, ungodly movies! What you feed your Spirit with is important.
- Watch less television, so that you can be vigilant and sober before the Holy Spirit at all times.

- Share your faith with unbelievers or non-Christians so that they can come to the saving knowledge of Jesus Christ our Lord.

As you flip over the leaves, get set for a transformation! You will become empowered to trust God and His Word more than ever before, belief in His promises to save, heal, deliver, restore, and bless you beyond your wildest imaginations!

# 2

✧

# FEAR

Fear is a tool of deceit wielded in the hands of the enemy. Some people have defined its acronym to mean a False **(F)** Evidence **(E)** Appearing **(A)** Real **(R)** in our lives. I stand to support the opinion that fear is unreal! Instead, it is the devil's stunts to pull and place you on the ground.

Whether you are experiencing fear in your life, work, family, or health, you must be aware that the negativity stems from the spiritual realm. Usually, the spiritual realm controls the physical. Doubt is introduced into the mind through a natural encounter, but it is fanned into fear by the operation of the demonic spirits.

Consider the wave of the COVID-19 pandemic which shook the faith of many across the world, leaving most vulnerable to the enemy. During the period, the evil one exercised the chance to permeate people's lives with unwanted sicknesses and diseases and losing their lives in the process. Matter of fact, a higher percentage of recorded death must have been riddled by its fear than its feel.

But here's the good news: a believer can superimpose the force of faith over the planes of fear and doubts. So, quit panicking or fainting, you have the power over the enemy by faith! The Scripture said that as a man thinks, so is he. (Proverbs 23:7)

Your boldness and confidence in God is the needed weapon for triumph over fear. When you activate your faith and take positive actions, you are automatically showing fear the doorway out!

### *What you must know about Fear*

- Fear cripples and imprisons.
- Fear brings about torments.
- Fear binds its victim.
- Fear sabotages the life of its victim.
- Fear births pains, sorrows, and sadness.

- Fear brings sicknesses and diseases.
- However, we can choose **Faith** over Fear now by the mercies and grace of Jesus Christ our Lord, Amen!

*What are you afraid of?*

*Is your fear, Cancer?*

*Is your fear, AIDS?*

*Is your fear, Lupus?*

*Is your fear, Mental illness, and Depressions?*

*Is your fear, Barrenness?*

*Is your fear, Sickle cell?*

*Is your fear, Ulcer?*

*Is your fear, Poverty, and the Lack of a Good Paying Job?*

*Is your fear, Leprosy?*

*Is your fear, Suicide?*

*Is your fear, Deafness, and Blindness?*

*Is your fear, Epilepsy, and Paralysis?*

There is hope for you today through Christ's redemptive blood! There is hope and solution through the power and Spirit of Jesus Christ. Even right now while you are reading, receive your healings and miracles by power and fire of the Holy Spirit in Jesus mighty name, Amen!

### *Choose Faith over your Fears!*

Choose your healing over sickness and disease. Opt for your deliverance instead of all oppressions. Believe in God for His miraculous deeds rather than the enemy for his dubious acts. Every time you are tempted or confronted by demons or the power of darkness, pray to God for faith over all fears in Jesus' name, Amen!

By the Spirit of God, there is a victory for you in the most critical circumstance. As you plead the blood of Jesus over your mind, soul, and spirit; every demon in hell, evil spirits, and satanic angels causing afflictions in your life will bow to you! They'll have all their nasty butt whooped right back into hell!

You need to understand that you're redeemed to live in sound health at all times. Infirmities and afflictions are not commonplace in your body, soul, or spirit. Rather, they belong to the burning hell! So, it's time to confront your fears in faith!

**Prayers of Faith over Fear**

- I plead the blood of Jesus over my mind in Jesus' name, Amen!

- Heavenly Father, I thank you for not giving me the spirit of fear but of faith over fear, power, and sound mind in Jesus' mighty name, Amen!

- LORD, thank you for paralyzing the demons of fear in my heart, mind, soul, and body in Jesus' mighty name, Amen!

- Arise O God, give me faith instead of fear and give me the grace to choose faith over fear, in Jesus' mighty name, Amen!

- Arise, O LORD, remove every affliction of sickness, disease, poverty, and pains caused by Satan and his demons in my life and body, in Jesus mighty name, Amen!

- Arise O LORD, let me be healed from every Cancer, in Jesus name, Amen!

- LORD, arise, remove the fear of COVID-19 from the nations of the earth, in Jesus mighty name, Amen!

- Arise O LORD, remove every demon of pain, affliction and disease from my soul and body, in Jesus mighty name, Amen!

- Heavenly Father, give me the grace to be victorious at all times and in times of crises of fear and doubts, in Jesus' mighty name, Amen!
- Arise O LORD, prosper me with wealth and riches, in Jesus mighty name, Amen!
- GOD, Arise and bless me with peace of mind from every fear, in Jesus' name, Amen!

# 3

✧

# FAITH WALK

*"For we walk by faith, not by sight"*

**2 Corinthians 5:7**

To walk by Faith is the opposite of walking by sight. When you walk by sight, you are only walking with the aid of your mind—your flesh. A fleshy walk exposes you to demonic activities and makes you susceptible to the attack of the enemy. However, faith walk is word walk by the Spirit's work.

## Meditate

*"All Scripture is given by inspiration of God, and is profitable for doctrine, for reproof, for correction, for instruction*

*in righteousness: That the man of God may be perfect, thoroughly furnished unto all good works."*
**2 Timothy 3:16-17.**

American clergy and author, Norman Vincent Peale advised, *"Change your thoughts and you change the world."* Closer to home, it would suffice to also change your world. Your thoughts move to influence decisions and affect your actions. See *Proverbs 23:7, Romans 10:9-10, Mark 11:24.*

To be inspired by the word firstly requires meditation of God's Word. What you ponder on becomes part of your life, spirit, soul, and eventually affects your body. Walking by faith means that you make good use of the insights and truths that settled in your mind in your time of meditation.

Ultimately, this means that you need to have God's word in your heart. I heard of a woman who struggled with putting God's word inside of her. So, she prayed to God to help her out and stamp His words on her heart. Then she got hold of a book that ministered an answer to her misery.

In the book, the author shared a story of how she had gotten out of a similar situation. While she studied, she wrote out the verses that struck her on sticky notes and note pads. She stuck a few on the refrigerator, bathroom mirror, and bedroom walls. Everywhere she went, she carried one or two index notes in her purse and prayed over herself with its content.

All scriptures are given to by the inspiration of God, so all scriptures are power-packed to deliver an overcomer's life to believers. Search the scriptures for relevant verses as it pertains to your area of concerns. Once you have steadied yourself in God's Word, begin to appropriate every divine insight that you receive and act on the word in faith.

## Follow

The Holy Spirit acts on God's word in our heart to bring about miracles. We can say that God's Word is self-sufficient and self-fulfilled because it is Spirit-energized! (Isaiah 55:1)

God's Word is categorized into two levels—the *logos* and the *rhema*. The Greek word, logos, refers to the constant and written word of God outlined in the Bible. It is the word of God we have in our hands.

Rhema is the lesser-known Greek word that refers to the instant, personal speaking of God to us. And this is the voice of the Holy Spirit. His voice may permeate our hearts as we ponder on the logos of God's word. It could come as a word of instruction, wisdom, or knowledge. Usually, it is characterized by God personally reaching out to us internally or externally.

God expects us to follow His leading by faith. When we walk following the dictates of His voice, He fills us with power enough to exercise faith over doubts. Your faith life is what gives you command and authority over the devil, death, and fear.

## Speak

What kind of miracle do you desire in your life? What are your aspirations, hopes, and expectations from the Lord? I have good news for you: everything you will ever need is already available in God's kingdom.

But it takes a conscious decision to obtain your heritage from the Lord. Consider what God said to the Isrealites in Psalm 81:10

*"I am the Lord your God, who brought you up out of Egypt. Open wide your mouth and I will fill it."*
He observed in verse 11.

*"But my people would not listen to me; Israel will not submit to me."*

God wants you to take (*listen to*) His words and proclaim it (*How? Opening your mouth wide*). When you speak God's word to the void atmosphere of sicknesses, stress, difficulties, and fear; He will fill the situation up with whatever you declared!

## Finally...

Your faith walk is the Word walk powered by the Spirit's work! And when you walk in faith, you become a terror to every form of fear that once hung around you.

# 4

❧

# OVERCOMING FEAR

*"For God hath not given us the spirit of fear; but*
*of power, and of love, and of a sound mind."*
**2 Timothy 1:7**

## Fear Is A Spirit

**F**ear cannot be defeated or removed by any psychological step or methodology. The spirit of fear can only be stopped by the power and grace of the Lord Jesus Christ. Amen! From the above scripture; The Bible indicates that Fear is not of God. But instead of the spirit of fear, God has supplied us with the Spirit of power, love, and sound mind. If you still manifest fear, you are walking out of your redemptive reality in

Christ Jesus. There is a need to retrace our tracks from fear right back to God's agenda of a faith-filled mind.

## The Place of Fasting

*"Howbeit this kind goeth not out but by prayer and fasting."*
**Matthew 17:21**

Fear robs believers of their faith and in turn their miracles. But the power of praying can subject every force of fear, especially when fasting is also employed. Usually, a time of fasting is a time of soul cleansing. Fasting is a Faith-move where we expect God to fill us with His Holy Spirit.

The apostle Paul reinforces the essence of our bodies in 1 Corinthians 6:19 when he questioned; *"Do you not know that your bodies are temples of the Holy Spirit, who is in you, whom you have received from God?"* (NIV) When we provoke the presence of the Holy Spirit through fasting, every demon of fear has no power to remain in our lives anymore.

Therefore, accompany your prayers with fasting. You may have to skip some meals on specific days of the week, each week. As you do this, you weaken the demon of fear from your mind, and the Spirit of God begins to reign in your life.

An important point to note is that you need to give yourself to prayers as you fast. Fasting without praying might get your body in shape, physically. But it may never immune you from being possessed by diverse forms of foul spirits. You need to make sure that you're filled with the Word of God and power as you fast. And how is this possible? Through praying while fasting!

Seriously, this is how to strongly choose faith over fear in all times and phases of life. Depending on God's Spirit to take the show is the way to overcome the strongholds of fear deposited by the evil one—the devil!

## Encouragements from the Scriptures

*"Be of good courage, and he shall strengthen your heart, all ye that hope in the LORD."*
**Psalm 31:24**

When the spirit of fear comes knocking, you need to wade it off by the words from the Scripture. You can always call on God in times of trouble and He will give you strength and victory over your fears!

## Prayers of Hope in God over the Spirit of Fear

- I cast down every tormenting spirit of fear in my mind in Jesus' mighty name, Amen.
- I destroy the demon of fear in my mind, soul, and body by the power of the blood of Jesus Christ, in Jesus' mighty name, Amen.
- I bind and destroy the strongman of fear in my mind and soul, in Jesus' mighty name, Amen.
- I receive hope and encouragement from God to overcome all fears, in Jesus' mighty name, Amen.
- I receive the grace and mercy from God over all fears, in Jesus' mighty name, Amen.

# 5

✣

# FAITH OVER FEAR

**Y**ou **can be fearless by choosing faith over your fears!** And it is possible to maintain an optimistic outlook on life and the future, always! Over the past months, I stumbled on a beautiful quote about being fearful or faithful. It read, *"Faith and fear both demand that you believe in something you cannot see. You choose!"*

As you wind through every circumstance, you can be assured to always meet with help to choose Christ's peace and faith with the help of the Holy Spirit. The scripture assured:

*"These things I have spoken unto you, that in me ye might have peace. In the world ye shall tribulation: but be of good cheer; I have overcome the world."*

**(John 16:33)**

Every time you focus on Christ, you are choosing faith over fear. You see, fear comes with unrest, but faith in God and His Word births everlasting peace. And what a joy! Jesus Christ is aware of our situations and can even feel it. (see Hebrew 4:15) He is also able to provide solutions to the problems of our lives right now!

Here's all you have to do: Surrender your heart, soul, and spirit to Jesus Christ and receive Him as your Savior and Deliverer. You'll notice how God's peace will flood your heart and wash over your troubles. Amen!

**Praises remove Fears**

Another way to choose faith over fear is through the force of praise and worship. Psalm 149:6 reveals that we wield a weapon in the battle against the enemy when we sing praises to God.

*"May the praise of God be in their mouths and a double edged-sword in their hands."*

Praise is likened to a double-edged sword. As we raise a song of praise to the Father, we are also rehearsing a shout of victory over the enemy at the same time.

Consider how praise can deliver us from the pit of fear in the following verses:

*"I will bless the LORD at all times; his praise*
*shall continually be in my mouth*

*My soul shall make her boast in the LORD: the*
*humble shall hear thereof, and be glad.*

*O magnify the LORD with me, and let*
*us exalt his name together.*

*I sought the LORD, and he heard me, and*
*delivered me from all my fears."*
**(Psalm 34: 1-4)**

## Confessions of Faith over Fears
## Say These Out Aloud:

- I confess that I have overcome all fears, doubts and anxieties, in Jesus' mighty name, Amen

- I confess that I am victorious over every demon of fear, in Jesus' mighty name, Amen.

- I confess that I have defeated the demon of fear through the blood of Jesus Christ shed on the cross of Calvary, in Jesus' mighty name, Amen.

- I confess that I have overcome all limitations and fruitless labors, in Jesus' mighty name, Amen.

- I confess that I am a winner over all fear; more than a conqueror through Christ Jesus, and victorious over all calamities of fears, in Jesus mighty name, Amen

- I confess that I am free from all demons and evil spirits of fear, in Jesus' mighty name, Amen.'

# 6

✦

# LETTING FAITH LOOSE

Faith is the only key that opens doors to God's miracles in the life of anybody and amid any condition. It is a life-saving power of God to revive any dying or death situation. In the middle of setbacks and failure, faith is the highway out into a world of success and breakthrough!

Like I earlier mentioned, faith is the sickle to draw your miracles from heaven to earth. *"Therefore, I say unto you, what things soever ye desire, when ye pray, believe that ye receive them, and ye shall have them."***(Mark 11:24)**

You can turn your faith loose for awe-struck move and miracles by your faith in God. When you turn your faith loose, God shows up, and only what God can do is permitted to come to play.

## The Place of Confessions in Miracles

*"For with the heart man believeth unto righteousness;*
*and with the mouth confession is made unto*
*Salvation. For the scripture saith,*
*"Whosoever believeth on him shall not be ashamed."*
**Romans 10:10-11**

There is absolute power in your tongue to release and turn loose all miracles that you want and need by faith.

*"A man's belly shall be satisfied with the fruit of his*
*mouth; and with the increase of his lips shall he*
*be filled. Death and life are in the power of*
*the tongue: and they that love it shall eat*
*the fruit thereof."* **(Proverbs 18:20-21)**

So, keep on seeking, asking, pressing for it until your desired door is opened. It definitely will be yours by faith!

*"Ask, and it shall be given you; seek, and ye shall find; knock, and it shall be opened unto you, for everyone that asketh receiveth; and he that seeketh findeth; and to him that knocketh it shall be opened."*

**(Matthew 7:7)**

What miracles are you believing God for? Just put your faith in line and trust Jesus that it will definitely be yours. Activate the commencement of that miracle by believing and throwing a praise and worship party to God and never a pity or fearful party.

# 7

✣

# FAITH THROUGH
# THE CROSS

The cross of Jesus reveals the truth about God to humanity. It exposes the depth of love that He has to every man—all sinners! Jesus suffered on calvary so that He would break the hold of fear off of the lives of many imprisoned by it.

Hebrew 2:14 to 15 captures an important purpose of Christ's death. The verse emphasizes, *"Since the children have flesh and blood, he too shared their humanity so that by his death he might break the power of him who holds the power of death—that is, the devil—and free those who all their lives were held in slavery by their fear of death."*

The cross of Jesus is the point of contact for victory from shame, pain, and fear. There is total liberty through the death of Jesus on the cross! Jesus declared on the cross; **"It is finished!"** The agony of fear is finally removed and eradicated by the cross of Jesus!

When Jesus resurrected from the grave on the third day and appeared to His disciples, He declared to them that: *"All power in Heaven and on Earth have been given unto Him."* And that includes the power of a sound mind instead of fear. Glory to God because this power is now available to all men through Jesus Christ! For, as the Father sent Him (Jesus), He has sent us in the same way! (John 20:21)

Dear friend, the ball is now in your court and the choice is now yours to remain in fear or walk out of it for life! By faith in the Son of God, we snuff out every jot of fear that exists in our lives. And when we call on the name of Jesus, every kind of oppression, hurt, and pain that stem from fear will fall flat on their faces.

Jesus has won the victory and so have you too!

**Pray these Powerful Prayers of Faith over Fear**

- I pray that I am delivered by the cross of Jesus and His shed blood from all fears, in Jesus' mighty name, Amen.

- I receive grace to always choose faith over my fears, in Jesus' name, Amen.

- I receive favor from God to choose faith through the cross of Jesus, in Jesus' holy name, Amen.

- I release the sword and fire of the LORD against fears, agonies and pains in my life, in Jesus' mighty name, Amen.

- I overcome all fears by the blood of Jesus, in Jesus' precious name, Amen.

- I confess that I live a victorious life over every Demon of fear, in Jesus' mighty name, Amen.

- I confess that I am totally set free and delivered from all fears, in Jesus' mighty name, Amen.

- Thank you, LORD JESUS, for making me overcome all fears in your precious name, and by your Cross, Amen.

# A CALL TO SALVATION AND REPENTANCE

✦

**J**esus Christ loves you and wants to save you. If you have not yet received or given your life to the Lord Jesus as your Lord and personal Savior, this is the hour, time, and day to do so. Maybe you are a backsliding Christian, this is the time to repent.

Repeat this prayer after me:

**DEAR LORD JESUS, I BELIEVE THAT YOU ARE THE SON OF GOD. I BELIEVE THAT YOU DIED ON THE CROSS FOR MY SINS, TRANSGRESSIONS, INIQUITIES, AND ABOMINATIONS THAT LEAD A MAN OR WOMAN TO HELLFIRE (PERDITION IN THE LAKE OF FIRE) AND YOU ROSE AGAIN ON THE THIRD DAY FOR MY JUSTIFICATION AND REDEMPTION. PLEASE, LORD, FORGIVE ME ALL MY SINS.**

**LORD, I CONFESS THAT I AM SAVED. WASH ME IN YOUR PRECIOUS BLOOD. I CONFESS THAT I AM BORN AGAIN. PLEASE LORD GOD, WRITE MY NAME IN THE LAMB'S BOOK OF LIFE IN HEAVEN, IN JESUS' PRECIOUS NAME I PRAY, AMEN!**

My dear friend, if you have sincerely said this prayer, believe you are now a new creation in Christ Jesus our Lord, Amen.

Get a copy of the Holy Bible and start reading from the book of John and the epistles of Paul the Apostle of Jesus Christ. Read Ephesians, Colossians, Galatians, Romans, and Hebrews, all in the New Testament. Also, join a Bible-believing church and start worshipping Jesus Christ, the Lord of Hosts. Amen!

Always remember that salvation or redemption is only through Jesus Christ the son of God. God loves you so much, Jesus Christ loves you! So, do I! Get my book **Victory in the Day of Personal Crises** on Amazon.com and **Barnes and Nobles.**

Please send me your Testimonies, Praise Reports, and Prayer Requests:

Evangelistbankole@gmail.com OR godliness1000@hotmail.com OR

Phone: +1 (917) 937-8944

Yours Sincerely in Christ's Service,

*EVANGELIST LIVINGSTONE OLALEKAN*

*BANKOLE, NYC, USA.*

*SHALOM!*

# AUTHOR'S PROFILE

ᐯ

Livingstone Olalekan Bankole is called by God as an Evangelist to take the saving gospel of Jesus Christ to the Nations of the earth through the Supernatural Power of God with miracles, healings, deliverances, and redemption of the nations of the world from sins, transgressions, iniquities, abominations, witchcraft, wickedness and the power of darkness. His main focus is the liberation and deliverance of people, tongues, tribes from the oppressions of Satan, his fallen angels, and demons of hell.

He is a student of Nyack College: a Christian School with a distinction. He is also a student of Pastoral Ministry. He is a graduate of Data Processing and Computer Networking and Security from Lagos City Computer College, Nigeria, and Anthem Institute Manhattan, New York City, USA respectively.

He is called to preach the undiluted and unpolluted word of God by the power of the Holy Ghost. Amen! He is happily married to OMONIYI BANKOLE and he currently resides in New York City, USA.

## Another Book By Same Author

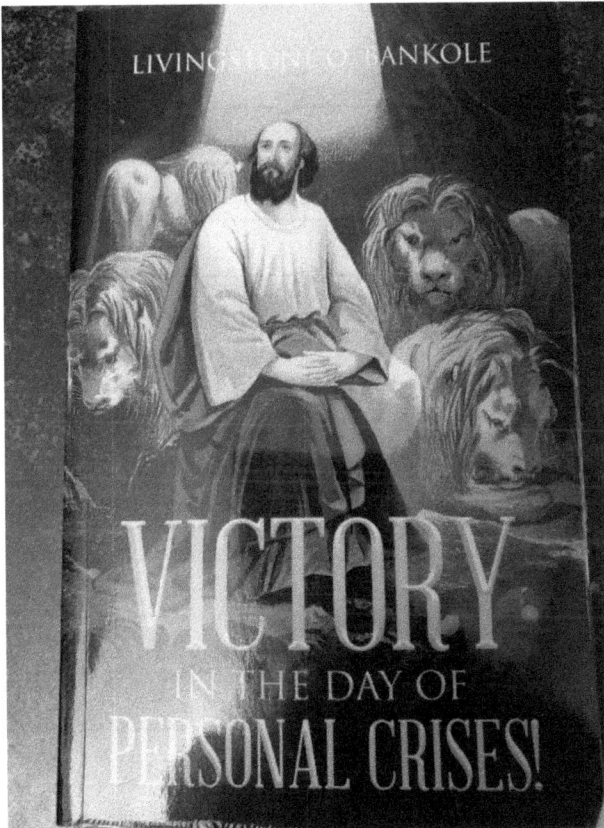

# NOTES

~

# NOTES

~

# NOTES

~

# NOTES

~

# NOTES

~